I0091430

SWIPE LEFT
SHOULD I STAY OR SHOULD I GO?

A humorous book of red flags in the dating world.
Looking for a trolley full of candy in a store full of Spam?
Searching for a bejewelled tuna in an ocean full of sharks?
I can help.

ASH LEE

Published by OMNE Publishing in 2021

Text © Ash Lee 2020

All rights reserved. No part of this book may be reproduced by any mechanical, photographic, or electronic process, or in the form of a phonographic recording; nor may it be stored in a retrieval system, transmitted or otherwise be copied for public or private use—other than for "fair use" as brief quotations embodied in articles and reviews— without prior written permission of the publisher.

A catalogue record for this book is available from the National Library of Australia

Cover Design	Andrew Akratos
Editing	Teresa Goudie
Internal Layout	Andrew Akratos
Photography	Perth Professional Photographers

Any opinions expressed in this book are exclusively those of the author and are not necessarily the views held or endorsed by the publisher. The names, places, events and identifying details have been changed to protect the privacy of individuals.

This book is available in print and Kindle formats.

CONTENTS

PREFACE

To all my ex-boyfriends who bought this book purely to see what I say about them: Thank you for your money. You will not see your name mentioned. There are no real names used in my book.

This book is not about airing dirty laundry; I even call myself out for being a dick in certain situations. Learning from your own experiences is essential to self-growth. I haven't merely examined my relationships with a fine-tooth comb and vomited that up onto a page. This book is about dating – the pre-relationship stage.

This book is what I wish someone had given 20-year-old me. I wish I had this guide to not only tell me what to expect from dating, but to also remind me what a great thing being single and independent can be. A resource to tell me that it's fine to want a partner; but you don't need one. Self-love and independence are more important because they will guide you on your journey to meet the right person.

To anyone reading this, please love yourself enough not to put up with crap from another person. I know I do. Not always, but now I do.

ACKNOWLEDGEMENTS

THANK YOU TO each fish I interacted with along the way, for giving me stories to fill this book with. Thank you all the shopping trolleys full of candy I have met who inspire me to continue to look for the right person.

Thank you to my friends who have supported me with every crazy book idea my ping pong brain has had, and said, "Yes, stick with this, it is good."

Thank you to those who have let me add their personal experiences into this book when I ran out of my own stories to include. Being able to use real experiences is very important to me.

Lastly this book is in loving memory of my dad, an educator if ever there was one. Christopher: 1954-2017.

INTRODUCTION

M Y NAME IS Ash. I am a pretty ordinary millennial girl trying to make my way through a confusing dating world. I have been single on and off throughout my twenties and the beginning of my thirties (I am 32 years old). I have been on an untold number of first dates and have been on both the giving and receiving end of not wanting a follow-up date. In my early- to mid-twenties I met men in bars and clubs, then the meat market selection moved to paid online dating sites (which I usually avoided paying for!), and now I use a dating site which is free, unless you want to pay for add-ons (which I have not yet done).

I'm not very social media savvy and had always hoped to meet someone in person. I had a dream of being on the bus when a good-looking, funny, smart, tall (please let him be tall) guy would ask me for the time, followed by a conversation, leading to a first date. Does this sort of stuff actually happen in real life? Other than being tooted at or called a cougar, *yes at age 32*, I rarely get approached by men. I am going to sound like an 89 year old saying this, and my friends will roll their eyes reading it, but I find that when I go out to socialise, so many people are on their phones. IT ANNOYS THE SHIT OUT OF ME! I don't care what you had for breakfast or who you can pretend to be for all of your followers. I care about the real world and real things.

I acknowledge that this book reveals a certain level of hypocrisy as I turn to social media platforms for my love life; diving into the world of gym selfies, borrowed dogs, borrowed children (e.g. nieces and nephews), shirtless photos and the list goes on. How can all us singles navigate our way through such shallow waters to find something a little deeper?

It is important to understand this book is not about having a successful relationship: I am currently single. This book is about avoiding an unsuccessful relationship right from the get-go. I want to teach you to pick up on all the warning signs I missed over the years. I am hoping to educate you by sharing real experiences, so you won't make the same mistakes. I am going to leave out any references to my long-term relationships as it would be too obvious who I am referring to and this ain't about shit-flinging. All the stories in this book are true; be it personal experiences or sourced from someone else, I have not made anything up. I'd also like to point out that I have been the tool in dating as well. I have led people on, I haven't always ended things in the way I probably should have, and there are ALWAYS two versions of the story. That said, I am going to share mine (with made up names).

ONLINE DATING:

Online dating comes in two forms and, as I believe both offer different experiences, it is important to differentiate between the two, so we know which kettle of barramundi we are dealing with.

Paid dating site: A dating site where a fee is paid in order to speak to other people on the site. Usually, whoever starts speaking pays the fee. There are also paid dating sites where all participants pay a fee to sign up. In the interest of full disclosure, I have never used the ones where exchanging money upfront was mandatory and because of that, I haven't included them in my book. It's clearly an expensive way to fish, but does it work? Who can say; you may bag yourself a damn good catch but how much will the bait cost?

Free dating site: A dating site that is (mostly) free. Extra options cost money but all parties can use it for free and chat with someone without paying if they wish.

I find that with free dating sites, you get more idiots because they don't care what they say as there are unlimited people to talk to and it's free to talk to all of them! This is where I got into conversations like this:

Horny Creep #1:	Hey, you like sex?
Ash:	Nah I hate it aye.
Convo ended.	

Ash:	Hey, how tall are you?
Guy changing the subject:	I'll tell you if you tell me your bra size.
Convo ended.	

Horny Creep #2:	Hey, you put out?
Ash:	Not for you.
Convo ended.	

With paid dating sites, I found more people were looking for a relationship than something casual. They were paying to try to find a connection, wanting something deeper than, "Hey girl, you hot." This isn't an absolute definite, but in my experience quite accurate. Please don't think this means that there are no crazies, or people who don't have your best interests at heart on paid sites too. There are still plenty of those sharp-toothed fish lurking in this ocean; it's your job to sort the wrong from the right and that's where this book comes in handy. You have to do this for you – nobody else is going to. Friends do give good advice … usually … if you have the right friends. Learn which of your friends to lean on; more about that later in the book.

ONE
RELATIONSHIP JUMPING

ELATIONSHIP JUMPING IS something I experienced in my early twenties. I wish someone had told me how detrimental it would be as I wore myself out learning this lesson. As the title itself suggests, it is when you come out of a relationship only to jump right back into another, then another, and another, and so on. You drain your energy fighting so hard to make relationships work that are simply wrong. Why did I do this? Why was it so important to me? I came up with the following:

1. I craved attention. Attention to me was acceptance and being accepted is all I ever wanted.
2. I didn't want to be alone. I was co-dependant, and I hadn't learnt to grow as a person, to appreciate the greatness that being independent could give me.
3. I didn't love myself enough to think I was worth more.

Dating to get attention. Saying this now in my thirties it seems silly, yet 20-year-old Ash wanted to be loved. That was the most important thing, no matter the cost.

If you are caught up in this phase, you're vulnerable and will likely attract the wrong sort of person. Attention is a superficial desire. Often people will say what you want to hear, in order to fulfil their own agenda. Someone may tell you that you're beautiful in order to have sex with you, for example. If they lay on the compliments thick and heavy enough and they get what they need, and you get what you need, where's the harm in that, right? WRONG. The attention is short-lived and superficial. If they make you feel special in that way so early on, imagine how many other girls/boys they do this to. A compliment that is genuine and truthful feels different to one that is superficial. Genuine compliments come from people who take the time to get to know you. If you like someone purely for superficial reasons, and they are doing the same, how long do you think that will last?

I am sure you are amazing; I know I am. I am worth getting to know, and you are too. Take your time getting to know someone, show them who you are, not just what you look like. While it's great to have that hot piece on your arm who constantly tells you how great your ass looks in those leather pants, don't you want him to tell you how smart you are too? Don't you want it to last longer than five minutes? Because if it doesn't, and you are still into relationship jumping, then … NEXT and repeat: shallow, bored, next, shallow, bored, next. Lots of girls look good in leather but YOU are the only you.

If you slow down and let yourself grieve after a relationship ends, and make yourself whole again, then you'll be ready for the next person who might just be the right one for you. But if you still have unresolved feelings for Person A, then Person B isn't going to make you get over him. Watching Person A move on with Miss Big-boobs Bimbo isn't any easier if you are dating someone you're just pretending to like. Also, in that case, you're being the tool because it isn't fair on Person B to be a mere be your distraction. This is where I have been immature and only realised it later. I did this a lot to people in my early twenties and even in my teenage years. Upon self-reflection, I was being a huge knob jockey and am glad I grew out of this phase.

After a break-up, you need to slow down, get out, see things, take a spontaneous trip, book it in, go! Go on your own. Travel, exercise, eat healthily and get some fucking clarity babe – it's the best thing you'll do. Then before you know it, you'll be over Person A and when Person B comes along and trips over, accidently spilling coffee all over your lap, you'll be able to laugh and wipe it up together.

TWO
BEING ALONE

S o many people fear being alone, worrying that they'll be the last person to settle down. Will there be anyone left for me, or will everyone else be settled down already? Thousands of fun questions to play on irritating repeat in your brain like a broken '60s record.

To start with, not everyone settles down with their high school sweethearts and, even if they do, it doesn't mean that it's forever. People grow at different paces, in different directions, and this is normal. Some couples grow together, some couples grow apart. It is a misconception that everyone is ready to settle down in their early twenties. The judgement you feel during those early relationships is usually imagined; it took me a long time to realise that for me, it was an internal voice judging me.

You can be single without being *alone*. Go out and see your friends. Start a new activity, meet people. Put yourself out there. Make sure you are the best and most amazing version of your lovely self before giving that to someone else. Because the truth is, if you're not the best version of yourself or you don't yet know who you are, chances are you may grow apart from whomever you meet.

One thing I can't stand is when I hear others say things like, "If that person is still single at their age there must be something wrong with them." Don't ever buy into this crap. Let's rethink this: If someone you know is saying that to you about another person,

ESPECIALLY if they're of a similar age, aren't they insulting you for being single as well? Implying that at your age (and you'd likely be looking in a similar dating bracket), if you aren't in a relationship there must be something wrong with you? I don't like the term, 'still single', because it feels like an insult or a threat. There is nothing wrong with being single; truthfully, it is amazing. Being in the right relationship is also amazing. Therefore, being single beats being in a crappy relationship, right?

So, if you think about it, people are always at different life stages: breaking-up, getting together, studying, travelling, baking millions of cookies, day-in-and-out. Even though the timing of when people are ready to commit to relationships changes, quality partners are always available when dating at any age, you just need to find them.

Another note I would like to add here is it may not only be you who is relationship jumping; it may also be the person you're dating. Something to watch out for. This is important because if you meet someone fresh out of a long relationship and they too have only been single for a few weeks, or a few months even, have they really grieved, self-discovered and healed? Could they be using you because they are too scared to be alone? Could they be using you to get over someone else? Make sure you tread carefully; no-one feels great being second best. Ask the right questions, but probably not on the first date as NO ONE likes talking about exes on the first date!

THREE
SELF-LOVE

FIRST OF ALL, this sounds corny because it is. You know why? Because sometimes, corny can be accurate. So here it is: With the exception of children (not the fur variety), you are the most important thing in your life. Until you put yourself first, you won't be truly happy in a relationship. If you cannot love yourself, why would someone else? You are responsible for you, so you need to learn self-love.

You need to learn to accept yourself and only then will others accept you too. And if they don't, then fuck 'em. If you accept yourself, who gives a vegemite-covered crumpet what anyone else thinks. A good way to grow and learn self-love is to travel to other places and experience different cultures, to open your mind to the possibilities of what else is out there. I am not talking about your annual trip to Bali, bogan-ing your way through six cartons of Bintang. I am talking about a unique experience: go see the Northern Lights; try to find the Loch Ness monster; go to the real Oktoberfest; see some art if you like; just do anything to open your mind to all the opportunities and experiences out there. You will find yourself along the way, and you will grow even if you go with a friend. You will learn how to be responsible for yourself and you *will* have fun.

Another way I discovered to create self-love is through achievement. Doing a university degree in something I loved gave me a sense of achievement, and every time I got a Distinction,

I was so proud. People around you may not display the same enthusiasm for your achievements but if it means a lot to YOU, then THAT is what is important. Learn something new and get good at it. Start small, walk before you run, and every time you get a little bit further you will appreciate yourself that much more. There are so many more ways to practice self-love; try a vibrator instead of your hands, for example, or treat yourself to a new brand of lube.

AUNTY ASH'S DOS AND DON'TS BEFORE A FIRST DATE

1. Don't put too high an expectation on a first date. If you go into every date thinking this could be my guy/girl and I could be the future Mrs/Mr Bejewelled Tuna, you will leave disappointed after a lot of those dates. I always like to prepare for a bad date, hopefully to come away pleasantly surprised. If you think every time is 'the time', then you are going to end up eating lots of tubs of ice cream.

2. If you're someone who gets really nervous before you go on a date, do some prep work! I don't mean flow charts and vodka shots – maybe have a few talking points prepared in case you get all flustered or run out of things to talk about. Quick true story: I once started dating a lovely guy and we hung out at his house. We wanted to Google something on his computer, and when he opened his browser, the site 'First date talking points' came up, and there was another called, 'How to catch your date's attention.' I thought this was adorable and showed a softer side to this man. A softer side to the ripped muscles and six-pack that appeared before me.

3. Take disappointment badly? Make sure you have some of your BFFs lined up for a post-date debrief. Even if it's just a cute little bestie call on the way home after things wind down.

4. I have a habit of dressing casually because I feel more comfortable. It is also a two-pronged way to catch the right fish. Not only are you comfortable, but you attract someone who likes you in your casually-dressed state. If you get to know cach other while you're relaxed and chill, can you imagine the look on his face when you finally wear a hot little number? It gives him a chance to like your personality, then he can be smacked in the face with your hot self when the sparks fly, and he has to try not to get electrocuted.

5. If you want to cancel on a first date for any reason, do it. Don't feel obligated: You're allowed to change your mind at any point for any reason. If you meet someone you really like one day, and have date with someone else the next day, just be honest. Everyone is looking for something and if you find it, it's okay to bail on other dates. What happens if you reluctantly go on the second date and that person really likes you? Wouldn't it be better not to put them through that head fuckery?

6. If you start to have doubts before the date, just tell them you're not keen (in a nice way). You haven't signed a marriage contract yet… so SWIPE LEFT….

FOUR
CHANGE

CHANGE IN TWO WAYS!

ONE: PERSONAL CHANGE

A NATURAL PROGRESSION IN life is growing and changing as a person. You ultimately decide what person you want to be. I changed multiple times before settling into the fine, albeit sarcastic, young lady writing this book. I remember when I was always negative and frequently relationship jumping. Two things happened to change these attributes, causing them to exit my persona as fast as a sale on selfie sticks causes teens to run from the house screaming all the way to the shops.

1. I was in Bali, walking along the beach with a group of friends towards a restaurant for my friend's birthday celebration. The sand was getting in my shoes and I was complaining about how much I hated sand in my shoes, and could someone carry me over a tiny stream so I wouldn't get my sandy feet wet? I had an epiphany. *Was I joking?* I thought. There were so many people in Bali who couldn't even afford to eat, couldn't afford to have more than one pair of shoes, or somewhere other than the beach to rest their head at night; and there I was complaining about sand in my shoes! It's true that I still hate sand in my shoes, it irks me 500%. BUT the takeaway

is that I stopped whinging so much after I heard myself constantly complaining about everything and realised what an unattractive quality it was. I hate it when other people complain, so why would people want to hear me complain? That was the beginning of me learning how to be positive, to speak positively, and to be empathetic to those around me, whilst still incorporating my amazing wit of course.

2. I let *the one* get away as a direct result of relationship jumping. I say *one* in italics because when it happened, it took me a long time to get over him yet in reality he probably wasn't right for me. We had been in a relationship for over a year and neither of us had said they loved one another, although when I look back our behaviour said it all. The disgusting, cringe-worthy longing glances were a dead giveaway. We started off as best friends and it evolved into a relationship. We broke up because I didn't think he wanted the same things as me, which was probably true especially at that time.

After the break-up I thought, *Yep, I am totally over that guy; he doesn't even want what I want anyways, time to move on.* So, I approached a guy I'd always been attracted to, and within a month I was dating him. It was a short-lived relationship and I realised I was, in fact, still in love with my ex. I wasn't being fair on anyone involved. I had stuffed things up with the first guy, who *had* been in love with me, but he just didn't know how to verbalise it. But do you think we could just go back? We tried, and were on and off again for a while, but too much had changed, and it didn't work out. A part of me always wonders if that was from the pain my relationship jumping had caused (or maybe my new-found sex skills weren't as mind-blowing as I thought). The answer is probably. Nobody wants to feel replaceable. It's definitely worth letting the dust settle before you move on; you don't know what feelings will resurface. In the meantime, use that vibrator and your new lube so the cobwebs don't close over your lady garden while you give yourself some space.

TWO: SOMEONE ELSE'S CHANGE

Now remember I am talking about the initial stages of dating – I have no idea what happens and what the rules are when people get married. (As already mentioned, I have not been in this position, nor am I willing to settle for anything less than the candy-filled delight of a man from my dreams.) What I do know is that you CANNOT make someone you are dating change their ways. Don't think otherwise – when you date someone it takes compromise. Part of dating is essentially accepting which of someone's bad habits you're willing to live with. To any boys reading this: Please put your toenail clippings in the bin. Also, LEAVE THE FUCKING TOILET SEAT DOWN. Both are deal breakers for so many girls.

The way they eat their cereal irks you; can you live with it? They smoke; is this a deal breaker? It is for me. I CANNOT and WILL NOT date a smoker; it is like acid to my soul. Everyone my age knows that smoking is bad for you and causes cancer. A smoker consciously chooses this form of self-harm which will one day burden their loved ones when they get sick. Even if you feel the same as I do, you must remember that regardless of your opinion, it is their choice to make. Your nagging them to quit every 30 seconds isn't going to make a light bulb go off in their head and they think, *oh yeah, I want to quit because I am being nagged.* You may spend months hounding this new partner, but it pisses them off, it pisses you off, there are no more snuggles and amazing new relationship bangs, and you eventually end it because, as you already knew, smoking is a deal breaker. Someone will only stop a behaviour because they want to, not because you want them to. The truth of the matter is, YOU chose to date

25

someone knowing they were a smoker, therefore that was a choice YOU made. They didn't take up smoking to piss you off, they were already doing it. If they wanted to quit, they would have quit. If not, they will hide it from you and do it anyway and your relationship will suffer. Personally, I wish we could put all the cigarettes in the world in a pile with all the Monopoly boards and have a giant bonfire. Future boyfriends take note: Monopoly-love is also a deal breaker for me. Like smoking, IT NEVER ENDS.

It is the same with drinking. If you don't like being around a heavy drinker, do not date one. I mean, nothing says 'do me' like the grotty morning-after smell of sweat and old booze, right? Trying to change someone is ridiculous and it drains the mojo out of your soul like nothing else. You have to choose the level of compromise when you start to date someone and assess if you're willing to put up with it. That annoying way they eat their cereal: yeah, I can live with that. I like the guy, but he smokes and drinks which I hate: NEXT! SWIPE LEFT!

I have been the inconsiderate jerk in this scenario so many times. This road leads to arguments, it leads to you feeling like you're someone's parent rather than their partner. Don't do it. Either you can live with their habits or you can't. If it is a deal breaker, then break that deal up-front before someone gets hurt or you're forced to play Monopoly: both scenarios end in tears.

FIVE
DATING DETECTIVE SCHOOL

OBSERVING

AFTER BECOMING THE wicked bitch that I am, I decided to break out some mad self-made social profiling skills to use in my dating (no matching degrees held). It's a three-step process people! These steps can also overlap each other. I hope that learning to observe gives you an easy way to tell if you're being shitted to by a bullshitter. Or if you are in fact the one doing the bullshitting and lying to yourself about the person.

VIEWING:

Now put on your non-creepy stalker detective hat and start the motor in your brain ticking please.

1. **Viewing Online:** The first obvious category to online dating is viewing. This one is important because it gives you an insight into the other person, or at least the version of themselves they want you to see. Men are usually holding a fish, flexing shirtless or cuddling a borrowed child or pooch for extra effectiveness. With online dating you need to be willing to accept that not everyone is truthful; you need to suss them out the best you can with the limited online information you have. I mean, seriously — is that dog even theirs?

With online dating this is hard to do. Usually, if someone is out to trick people, they have put a lot of thought into it. Profile trickery comes in many forms which I will discuss later in this book; but a few examples to mention now are when they lie about their education, job, family, appearance (yes, I consider this a lie too), hobbies and personality.

This next point can come under either viewing or hearing so when you read someone's profile, take note. If someone says they don't want children or they aren't sure what they want, and you're keen as a bean to settle down and pop out babies like burgers at a fast-food place, then swipe left. You cannot and do not want to push someone into changing their mind. Truthfully, you are going to waste both of your time. Not knowing what they want may mean they are between relationships; in that case I guess you could meet up to see if there is some crazy connection that leads to them being your soulmate. If that crazy connection isn't there, though, I wouldn't bother. It is a head fuck; and not the type that feels good.

Again, same logic: If the person you're interested in isn't active and you want to date someone sporty, you cannot force them to enjoy your activities. You can introduce them or lead by example, but you cannot pressure or force them to change. That isn't exactly the best way to enter a relationship. Essentially, you're telling the other person they aren't good enough as they are... it's not like you can slowly change and mould him into Ryan Gosling. Either you're dating Ryan Gosling or you're not, and I'm going to go out on a limb here and assume that you're not, so you need to accept the person you're with.

2. **Viewing in Person:** Viewing is fun at pubs – and by viewing, I mean perving. When I like a guy, I watch him and try to work out if he is single. I look for any sign that he might be interested in me. If you like someone and they smile at you,

DO NOT LOOK AWAY. Smile back, gorgeous! Interaction starts there: Even if you are lobster-red from smiling back, at least you're communicating with them. When you view them, make sure you consider their attitude and behaviour if possible. Are they on the prowl for a hot lay, or something more? Are they just looking to chill with mates? Are they making eyes at every other person, or just at you?

LISTENING:

Okay time to use those things on the side of your head, your ears. They aren't just there to look pretty, covered in your latest sparkly dangles. Sound and words; it's called science.

3. **Online Listening:** When you speak to someone and they sound genuine, make sure you listen to what they are telling you.

- "I don't want kids," from someone genuine means they don't want kids.
- "I don't want something serious," means they don't want something serious.
- "I don't like sharing meals," means no tapas … get it?

If you can tell they are genuine and don't want what you want, and you aren't willing to compromise on not trying your partner's food, then you can't be with them. If someone said they wanted to play Monopoly with me every day for the rest of our lives, no deal. I would send him straight to jail without passing go or collecting two hundred dating dollars. Time to dive back into the ocean to keep looking for that elusive bejewelled tuna.

Sometimes people tell you things subtly, or say them in a roundabout way, or don't say them at all to avoid tension. Ask direct questions so there is no confusion (not necessarily on a first date but within the first few dates). I don't think there is anything wrong with knowing what they want in life. While I don't advise saying, "I want ten kids with you named, Betty, Dawn, Fraser, blah, blah, blah," definitely find out if having kids is something they see in their future. If you have the travel bug, you should ask them, "Do you want to travel or live overseas?" There is nothing wrong with this to set you on the right track. I find it is good to do this before there are any strong feelings, so ending things won't leave you overly emotionally affected. Then you can bow out and protect yourself before it is too late and you find yourself lying on the floor listening to Leona Lewis' *Bleeding Love* or Brandy's *Have You Ever* – my high school go-to songs of wah times.

4. **Listening in Person:** Observe how they talk to those around them. Are they behaving like a horny teenager, drowning in Lynx deodorant and excess hair gel, looking for someone, anyone, to fuck? Or are they not looking for anything and happen to stumble on you (not in you) as a lovely surprise? If someone is out looking for sex, chances are they just want sex. It *could* lead to something else. It could not. Relationships don't grow on trees; you find the fish in the sea. Obviously.

ANALYSING:

5. **Analysing in Person:** I like to observe a person's physical behaviour towards me, so I can judge how they feel about me. I can usually feel when someone is into me. Not everyone is an affectionate person but everyone has a tell: Whether it is a romantic glance or a touch on the arm, or if they laugh at your jokes, especially the terrible ones where you fuck up the punch line. Are they nervous around you? Do their words not seem to come out straight when they talk to you? Because that is adorable. If someone is standoffish, especially after the first kiss or hook up, I'd be betting they aren't sure what they

want. Are they courteous to others at the bar? Are they polite to waitstaff? If they are pushy and nudge people out of the way I'd probably leave that bull in the china shop and move along. NEXT.

AUNTY ASH'S IMPORTANT RULES FOR A FIRST DATE

1. Absolutely under no circumstance get into a car with someone on the first date.

2. Always meet in a public venue. Be cautious and make sure there are others around if your date walks you back to your car.

3. Don't give your date your mobile number up front – they can use social media and get more personal information than you want them to. Get their number so you can sit on it (not literally) to decide if you want to see them again before messaging.

4. Always, always, always, regardless of how low-key and how much you have chatted to this person, keep your serial killer radar on in the back of your head. Screen shot all details to your bestie (to whom I will refer as your safety person throughout the book). Do this the first few times you meet your date and especially the first time you go to their house or any secondary location with them.

5. If you haven't already, download a tracking app on your phone and share it with your safety person and family member/s.

SIX
DECIDING ON A FIRST DATE MEET UP

THIS SECTION BRINGS me to a few funny stories I personally experienced pre-meet up. I choose to laugh at them now; some of you might get upset about the way I was spoken to. I look at them as lessons from the dating gods for helping me dodge epic bullets of dissatisfaction from being shot through my heart, rather than one of Cupid's love-coated arrows.

STORYTIME:

This is one super doozy of a story. I am grateful that, on the whole, I know what I am about and what I am willing do in my life to get what I want. I'm not saying I know what I want in every instance but, when I do, just try and stop me from getting it: I am one fierce bitch.

So I was on a paid dating site, and this *nice* guy, whom I am going to call Bertie for the purpose of this story, had a *nice* profile and he expressed that he would like to talk to me. I reciprocated the interest at that stage. He began talking to me, which would have cost him money. As soon as we began chatting, I knew that I would never meet up with him. He sent three messages to my one, and if I was online and had not yet replied, he would send another message. I knew I would be wading in potential serial killer waters if I met up with him — or more likely someone super-needy with possible control issues.

I wanted to be polite, as I knew he had paid to speak with me, so I continued chatting beyond the first few interactions. I kept my replies short and boring and hoped he wouldn't be interested in catching up either (which must have been hard because obviously I am hilarious). One thing led to another, my humour and amazingness had clearly seeped of out my pores, through the computer and into the guy by some weird digital osmosis, and he asked to meet up with me. The conversation then followed something like below:

Bertie: Would you like to catch up for a coffee with me?

Ash: Thank you so much for the offer; I feel like we don't have a similar sense of humour. I wish you all the best meeting the right chick that you have lots in common with.

No reply despite receipt showing it was read one millisecond after I sent it. Two days later:

Bertie: Well I see you obviously haven't found someone with a similar sense of humour, whatever that even is, ha.

I replied, against my better judgement, as his tone did not please me, and the conversation continued:

Ash: No, it has been only two days, and I am happy to keep waiting until I find someone I feel enough of a connection with to catch up with them.

Bertie: You'll probably just stay single; you're getting older and your ovaries will dry up.

Ash: That is fine, my ovaries can dry up if they please. I would never settle down just to have children because that is a terrible idea. If I don't meet the right person, I won't have kids. No stress. Also, I'd like to mention you are six years older than me.

Bertie: This is exactly why there are so many single mums out there. This kind of attitude.

I then rolled my eyes at the fact that my point was the direct opposite of being a single mum, whilst also thinking *so what if people are single mums if they are happy?* So, I responded with:

Did you ever stop to think that for every single mum out there, there is also a single dad? When did it become the woman's fault for becoming single? Why is the woman the only one responsible for the child in your fantasy situation? Lastly, I would like to thank you Bertie, for proving to me I made the correct decision in not meeting up with you. I hope your semen doesn't dry up while you're looking for the right person. Lucky girl that will be.

And then I blocked him. I felt pleased with the progression of the situation. Some women in that situation might have thought, "Is he right? Am I running out of time?" I didn't look at it that way and look at it now gratefully. I don't put pressure on myself to meet the right person. I know that science has progressed so far that if I am desperate to be a mum then artificial insemination is an option. And probably cheaper than having a nasty divorce.

TAKEAWAYS:

1. Trust your gut. If the person feels a little off to you, regardless of whether they have paid to speak to you or not, don't meet up with them.
2. Don't let someone put an [egg] timer on your ovaries. Don't listen, things will happen as they do, not as some ass wipe

dictates them to you. Unless it is your doctor, in which case I'd listen to their ovary advice for sure; they know sciences and stuff.

3. I would say don't challenge someone, but I'd be a hypocrite because I totally put this guy back in his box and there was no way he was going to be allowed in my box. I was feeling feisty that day; usually I would have blocked the guy straight away after he came back with his smartass comment about not meeting anyone roughly 12 seconds (two days) after we last spoke. Challenging someone isn't really the smartest option as they could lash out. This guy had a very warped opinion of women already and I could have easily provoked him. Blocking is the easiest and safest method; however, I am glad I didn't do that, or I wouldn't be able to share this story with you.

4. Desperation: I have said it once and I'll say it again. GROSS. If they are sending you 56 messages to every one message you send, just rule them out.

5. Just because they paid doesn't mean you owe them a date. I am very repetitive on this point throughout my book and it is intentionally so. It took a long time to train myself out of that belief. I am repeating it for both your benefit and mine so my grasp on the concept doesn't drizzle out of my nose the next time I have a cold.

6. BLOCK, BLOCK, BLOCK the shit out of them. Take that. Boom.

STORYTIME:

In this next story, although there was fuckwittery on both sides, I was the main culprit. I was on a paid dating app, chatting to a guy and the conversation was a little *off*. His spelling was bad, and he claimed to be a semi-professional sports star as well as working elsewhere. He didn't ask me any questions, he just continued to talk about himself (with lots of typos) throughout our exchange. I was going to write the guy off as someone who was catfishing, something I hadn't previously experienced. Then my curiosity got the better of me and I decided to investigate. My housemate agreed that the upside-down and weird symbols peppered throughout our conversation were possibly from a foreign keyboard.

I put my detective hat on (I was in my pyjamas) and found that all the photos on his profile were locatable on Google. As the guy had dropped his full name almost immediately (which I found suspicious; he clearly wanted me to know who he was) I was able to Google this too. At this point, instead of simply deciding to leave it alone, I dug deeper. I found his profile on social media and chuckled to myself because all the photos from the dating app were on his profile as well as Google. He was clearly a fraud: This was where the catfish got his stolen images from.

I DM'ed the semi-professional sports person (SPSP) and it went something like this:

Ash: Hi, sorry if this is weird but I thought you should know someone has stolen your images and started a fake online dating profile. The person can't spell at all, he even made typos in the supposed suburb he works in. Did you want me to keep up the act while you investigate and take action?

SPSP: Um, that *was* me. I thought that was how you spelt it?

Ash: Oh, I am so sorry. We can continue chatting on there if you like.

Weirdly, the guy didn't seem offended. He also didn't see

the humour in it (I wouldn't have either). He came across as completely impartial. I ended up meeting with him as a guilt date for the way I had behaved. As I thought, he spent the whole date talking about himself, and also displayed bad manners over dinner.

He complained about his steak and said that if he were at home and this had been cooked by his mum, he would have told her it was bad and asked her to recook it. He then claimed I wouldn't be able to beat him at air hockey because he was too good at sports. He wasn't saying it as a joke; he was dead serious. I beat him. He tried to blame everything but himself on losing the game. There was much, much more to this story, including his misogynistic views, but I think I have covered enough ground here. Basically, NO DEAL. I went on a guilt date and all I got was a soggy steak that went into the bin when really all I wanted was candy. Ditch the soggy steak back and keep swiping those luscious fingers until you uncover some CANDAAAAAAAAAAAAAAAY!

TAKEAWAYS:

1. Don't jump to conclusions too quickly: This one's all on me. I should have been nicer in the way I approached it. Sometimes even when you are completely sure, you can be wrong.
2. Be nice on social media. Recognise that sometimes people spell poorly and have bad grammar but that doesn't mean they're not smart. Don't judge someone purely on the way they write, especially if it is me or I am heading straight to hell, do not pass go do not collect $200.00.
3. Trust your gut. If you don't want to go on a date, then don't. This goes back to owing someone something. I felt like I owed him a date because of my behaviour. Really, I should have accepted and apologised for being rude and left it at that.

STORYTIME:

This story is a doozy – a crazy doozy of a meeting and series of events that followed. Still to this day, this story sounds fake because it is just that stupid. I was out with some close friends at a pub on a Sunday evening celebrating some event or other. Obviously, I was looking fab and although years have passed, I remember I was wearing my cute little blue dress with the cut outs on the back. Anyways. At the pub and a guy, whom I will call Alfonzo, caught my eye from across the room. He saw me, I saw him. I walked past him as I went to the loo and when I smiled, he smiled back. Soul mates, right? Don't get too excited.

I was sitting back down with some guy friends and Alfonzo struts up to see if he can buy me a drink. *He had big balls*, I thought, *probably literally too*. I agreed. He was chatting to me and my mates as were a few of his older work buddies. Turns out he was a real estate agent. Obvious career choice if you consider both his heightened confidence and the amount of hair gel he used. Then I wanted to go and hang out with a few of my girlfriends who were sitting outside. I gave him the old, "Hey I am here with friends so maybe I can give you my number and we can catch up at a later time," spiel. Which is code for: I am here with friends and you're cute but fuck off. For now.

Well, he messaged me roughly 30 times before I even left the pub because he wanted to take me out that night. He wanted to hang out, he wanted all those things. I declined repeatedly and said, "We can catch up at a later date." He came and gave me a kiss goodnight – it was a nice kiss – and I thought, *If only I can teach this guy to calm his farm it could turn into something*.

Alfonzo called me after work one night that week, and I thought that was okay. Despite sending too many text messages, I was actually enjoying the attention. We were having a nice chat on the phone and the conversation went as follows:

Ash: It's been nice chatting with you, but I have netball, so I have to go.

Alfonzo: Oh, I watch netball sometimes, it's quite a good sport.

Ash: Yeah, it's addictive. Who do you watch play netball?

Alfonzo: My girlfriend.

Ash: Like your friend who is a girl, or your girlfriend, girlfriend?

Alfonzo: No, my girlfriend.

Ash: [Takes a long pause, followed directly by another long pause] You have a girlfriend?

Alfonzo: Yes.

Ash: How can you even be pursuing me? This is a joke!

Lots of yelling at him, calling him a jerk and millions of inappropriate words followed. I won't repeat them but please feel free to use your imagination. I also requested he delete my number and never call me again.

I was shocked. People do this? Why? Why bother dating someone if you are going to chat up other people? Be single if you aren't fully committed to your relationship. Being single is amazing, why let go of that for someone you don't care about? I felt awful for his girlfriend and sick for days afterwards about my accidental part in the situation.

You would think that was where the story ends ... YOU WOULD THINK. It wasn't. I ignored several calls from Alfonzo throughout the week. The weekend arrived and I was having after-work drinks with my lovely colleagues again, *totally not a big drinker*. My phone rang; it was a private number. I answered because my dad was living in China at the time and whenever he called me, it showed up as a private number. Rookie mistake. The voice on the other end of the line was some guy who sounded like he was in his 50s, *yet it wasn't my dad*:

John: Hi Ash? My name is John. I met you the other night with Alfonzo.

Ash: Hi … ummmm okay?

John: Alfonzo has explained to me what happened and wanted me to give you a call to see if I can set something up between you two. He is very sorry and has broken up with his girlfriend. He really likes you and wants to take you out.

Ash: Well John, I have been ignoring Alfonzo's calls for a reason. Why would I date anyone who set out to cheat on their partner with me? How do I know he wouldn't do the same thing to me one day? It isn't a very good start for dating is it?

John: No, I guess not.

Ash: Please tell Alfonzo not to call me again, not to have his friends call me again, not to text me, not to email me, not to send a carrier pigeon.

Finally, this is where this story ends, *about ten steps too late*. In fact, a whole story too late as it should have never begun. Can I blame my cute little blue dress? No, I can't. This was purely Alfonzo's fault and I had zero responsibility for his behaviour.

TAKEAWAYS:

1. Real estate agents (among others). Always be wary of those who wear excessive amounts of hair gel and take way too long in front of the mirror getting ready.

2. Never give someone your number – always get theirs so you can control the initial messaging.
3. If someone messages you more than once or twice an hour after an initial meeting, when you are still in the same venue, it's a good sign they are needy.
4. Listen to social cues on the phone and don't be scared to ask if something doesn't make sense.
5. You can never know someone after one meeting. They could hide things and be someone completely different to the way they initially portrayed themselves. Unfortunately, it's unlikely they are going to be Spiderman to your Mary-Jane.
6. If you end contact with someone you were dating and you start getting calls from a private number, don't answer. If there is someone in your life who calls you from a private number, ask them to message or email you before they call. Until the crazy stalker calling ends.
7. Don't ever blame your appearance for someone else's behaviour. People can be assholes and it is certainly not your fault. Wear that dress with pride and confidence.

STORYTIME:

My friend, whom I am going to call Walter, had a date with a guy he'd met on a free dating website and they really hit it off. The conversation was great, and Walter was super excited to meet up with him. He was crushing so much he got a new outfit and a haircut. *Lame, but totally cute.*

Walter sat and waited for his date to pick him up. 15 minutes passed. 20 minutes. 30 minutes passed. As Walter flicked through his favourite episodes of Gilmore Girls, he received a text message. It was the date, I'll call him Floyd, who told Walter that he was expecting a delivery at around 7:00pm so he couldn't come anymore. Walter was a little confused; why would anyone be delivering parcels on a Saturday night? Why did that mean the date could no longer take place? Walter asked Floyd if his housemates could sign for the parcel instead. That was when the communication stopped. Floyd just didn't reply to Walter. End of story.

TAKEAWAYS:

1. Don't expect too much from someone you don't know. If you don't have high expectations, you won't be too disappointed when they don't deliver.
2. If someone is going to cancel on you for a stupid reason, this is an example of their poor manners and they are probably not worth hanging out with anyway.
3. The only thing I would have done differently was perhaps call him out on his bad manners, *if I was feeling particularly obnoxious that night,* even though I am not sure the moron was worth the energy.

STORYTIME:

I have merged a few stories together here which have a common theme and happened to some of my girlfriends. They met guys on paid dating sites, and soon started dating and getting to know one another. It was nice, they hung out and got all intimate and Lusty McLustface with one another. Then my friends started to get nagged for sex without protection. This sort of behaviour is totally unacceptable, and it has also happened to me many times. What is particularly annoying is how common it is. The guys want sex without protection... WHEN THEY DON'T EVEN

KNOW YOU. And if you don't agree to it, they seem to think that continuing to nag will wear you down.

I imagine on some, maybe more impressionable, girls it would work. Whenever it happened to me I felt like I had to justify my position by saying, "I'm not on the pill" or, "I feel like that is a long-term relationship thing once both of us get tested." Every refusal was met with a plea to reconsider, with reasons why I was wrong, or why it would be fine. You shouldn't have to explain yourself to any guy or girl. Saying no to something you aren't comfortable with should be the end of the discussion, not the beginning of constant pleas that make you feel wrong or prudish.

TAKEAWAYS:

1. Be firm on birth control. If you aren't on the pill and you are worried about getting pregnant or STDs (which we should all worry about), it is your responsibility to make sure you are preventing this by insisting on condoms or other similar protection. DO NOT let someone else tell you what is or isn't okay for your body. Just because someone else might not have fallen pregnant that way doesn't mean you won't. Also, you don't know if he has an STD, or if someone else he had sex with has an STD, or how many people he convinced to have unprotected sex with him before you. Get my point? GOOD.

STORYTIME:

A guy I was getting to know asked me for nude photos. I laughed it off at first and let him know that I had never, and would never, send nude photos. I will go my entire life without sending nude photos. Firstly because I don't want to, and secondly because one day, if I have kids and they want to do stupid shit like this and tell me that I did it too, I can say, "Uh, I did not".

He asked about three times in total for nude pictures and the last conversation was the one that made me decide I was done:

Guy: Send nudes.

Ash: [Sick of constantly saying no, thought I'd try a new approach] I will send you a nude if you send me one of you first.

Guy: Why? Everyone knows that a woman's body is more attractive than a guy's.

Ash: Well, I'm not attracted to girls, I'm attracted to guys. So, if you go ahead and send one through to me, I'll send one back.

Guy: I can't. It's difficult.

Ash: How is it difficult?

Guy: It is difficult in the sense that I don't wanna do it.

Ash: So, you don't want to send a photo of yourself naked, yet you still expect me to?

No response, come back, or reply.

Later on, he asked me out for dinner. I called him and said I wasn't into it. There were also other 'not over the ex' issues I'd picked up on. Pile all issues on top of each other and you get a big steaming pile of a shitty way to start a relationship.

TAKEAWAYS:

1. If you don't want to send nude pics, don't. Simple.
2. If someone isn't over their ex, don't waste your time. NEXT.
3. If you are not comfortable with something sexual, saying no once should be enough. You don't have to repeat yourself.

You don't have to justify your decision. Don't let someone try to determine what is acceptable for you. The truth is, even though I didn't know this guy for more than a few weeks, what I DID learn quickly was that he would try to talk me into something I wasn't comfortable with; ultimately that is why I ended things. Who knows who he would have shown those photos to and where he would have posted them, had I sent any.

STORYTIME:

This story is another from my friend Walter. This time he met someone through social media, not a dating site. They agreed to meet up, and the guy, whom I will call Norman, was coming up from Mandurah to hang with Walter in Perth. That's a good one hour-ish trip (I personally wouldn't bother because I am lazy) so hats off to Norman and Walter for arranging to meet up.

Norman told Walter that he was running a little late, so there was an open line of communication which is always handy. One hour passed. Walter paused Gilmore Girls and noticed he was very late, not just a little late. He started to wonder what had happened to Norman. He sipped on his coffee as he watched Dean break up with Rory and thought, *well he did say he would be late*. Then, when Dean broke up with Rory for the second time, Walter paused the TV again and noticed it had been one and a half hours. He was starting to get worried so at that point he sent Norman a message. There was no reply. Walter got back into Gilmore Girls and waited, a little worried as per his empathetic personality. Two hours passed and FINALLY Rory and Jess got together, but that's not all … Norman finally messaged Walter! He let him know that his tyre went flat halfway to Perth, so his dad came to help sort it out. Walter said, "No problems that you're late, when are you getting here?" Norman replied that he went home after the tyre was fixed. End of communication. End of story. (By the way, Jess and Rory don't last either, spoiler alert.)

TAKEAWAYS:

1. Manners, people! Communication doesn't hurt right? The guy was halfway there and, while he was stuck waiting for his dad, he had time to send a text.
2. Also, be empathetic. It was a weird situation; Norman may have been going through more than a flat tyre … maybe?

SEVEN
THINGS THAT PUT ME OFF
DURING FIRST DATES

I N THIS CHAPTER I am going to continue to play storyteller. Let's run through some irky things I experienced on first dates that put me off from going on a second date.

STORYTIME:

I had been chatting with a guy for a while on a free dating site. We both put off meeting each other for various reasons and when we finally met up, he was not at all what I was expecting. Sometimes this can be a good thing and I am pleasantly surprised, and sometimes this can be a bad thing and I want to get home ASAP, get into my pjs, curl up in bed and eat a fuck tonne of chocolate. So, back to my date. This was one of the occasions where I was in no way pleasantly surprised.

The guy drained my energy, which I usually have a lot of. He asked question after question, only giving me half a moment to reply. His laughter felt fake, it was loud and robotic, and his responses seemed rehearsed and ingenuine. He was completely over the top with my dog, giving her commands which really pissed me off. He kept making her come to him to be patted when she clearly just wanted to walk, but he was insistent, and she was confused. Don't mess with a person's dog on a date. You'll come out second best aye.

All of these things were noted, but the real red flag came after he discussed his upcoming holiday overseas. When he mentioned the country he was going to, I said, "Cool, I have always wanted to go there, I'm jealous!" I felt like that was quite a normal response. His response, however, was ten steps beyond what I'd consider normal. In fact, it was more like ten leaps … minimum.

He very seriously said, "Well you should come. Book your leave and do it."

I politely said, "No it's not a good time for me."

"Why not? It will be good, do it." He harped on and on, urging me to come with him at least four times in five minutes. It was like when he insisted that my dog, who didn't want to be patted, come to him to be patted. NO! Get a life – who would even agree to do that? Guy would probably propose on the trip with boundaries like those.

As the date was approaching its end, and seeing he was a doctor, I wondered (knowing full well I wasn't going on a second date with him) whether I could ask him if a mole on my arm was cancerous. He was a doctor, after all, and I was too lazy to go to my usual doctor.

The answer is NO, do not do that! You become the problem person on the date if you pull this crap. Book an appointment, go to a doctor, and get your moles checked properly people! Do not take or ask for services from your date. Pay someone to mow your lawn, pay someone to service your air conditioner, pay someone to wash your adorable big-eyed drooling dog. You don't want to feel you owe a stranger any favours.

Some people are so desperate to find a relationship that they try to manufacture it. Perhaps he was pretending to be spontaneous, but I took it as him being too intense when I didn't even know him. What was interesting though, was that I thought he'd be one of those guys who would hit me up with continuous messages asking me for another date. Instead, later that same day, he unmatched me on the dating site. My thoughts on this: He will continue to go on first dates between now and his holiday until he finds someone desperate enough to accept his offer to go overseas with him. Those two will then live desperate inauthentic lives until one of them realises that they didn't even know the other person because they were both pretending the whole time.

TAKEAWAYS:

1. Use your intuition to see if someone is being their authentic self. This guy was acting and was really full-on. The laugh was very fake and inappropriate at times, and the way he acted with my dog was not genuine.
2. Just because someone has a good job, like a doctor, doesn't mean you should latch onto them.
3. Making a ridiculous suggestion like going on a holiday, or what your kids would look like, or meeting their parents on a first date, is a RED ALERT! CODE RED! Seriously, just walk away and face palm, then head over to the supermarket and get whatever chocolate you need to make the gross feeling go away.
4. Desperation is disgusting on a date. You can smell it from a mile away … with your ears because it is something you hear and interpret, not something you smell as the saying goes.
5. Just because someone you meet has a job that provides a service you need; it doesn't mean you can ask them to provide this service for you. You don't want to feel you owe a favour to that person. This will affect your subconscious into giving them a second date, even if you don't want to. You should never owe anyone anything EVER! Unless you borrow money from them, then you legit owe them money.

STORYTIME:

I went on a first date with a guy whom I will call Stanford for this story. Stanford was new to Perth and was opening up a store, which he liked to brag about, with his supposedly silent partner, whom he named five minutes into the date. He liked to drop unsubtle hints about his financial situation and showed me the receipt of a six-figure sum of money he'd lent to his sister. Why? Well that is something I wish I'd asked myself on the date but instead I thought about it later.

I went to give Stanford money for our dinner, but he wouldn't let me contribute. Don't get excited though – he also chose what we ate. We had some share platters and he put food onto my plate for me, but not in the cute way like in movies. As we sat and ate, quite close to each other might I add, he reached under the table and dragged my chair closer to his. Perhaps he thought I was a toddler? Thankfully, I didn't have steak that needed cutting. (Although I did manage to sausage block him all by myself.)

I told Stanford how I was trying to get into the police force – thank fuck I didn't get in – but at that time I was trying hard. I had trained and trained and done lots of study. One of my main reasons for wanting to get into the force was the interesting nature of the everchanging role and being physically active and not having to sit at a desk from nine to five everyday like in my job at that time. Directly after this conversation, Stanford mentioned that there was a job going at his new workplace for a receptionist, hinting that I might suit this role. *Did he even listen at all?*

After dinner, we decided to go for a walk to get some coffee (Stanford's decision). I continued to listen to his stories about how amazing he was and how much money he had and how unique he was [*yawn*]. We got to the coffee shop and I said, "I'll pay for the coffee, as you got dinner." He laughed, and said patronisingly, "Well if you're sure you can afford it."

As he walked me back to my car, he asked if I was free both Friday and Saturday nights to see him. I said I would see him again on Friday night, knowing I could get out of it later. "What, are you catching up with your other boyfriend on Saturday night?" he teased. 32-year-old Ash would never put up with this. 23-year-old Ash let the comment slide.

Stanford sent me texts that night and tried calling me the next day. I texted him back, told him I didn't feel the spark, and that was it. Done. I felt disgusting about the date for weeks after. I couldn't work out why at the time. As I got older, I realised how many asshole alerts I had missed on that date. Complete fuckwittery at its finest, seriously.

TAKEAWAYS:

1. If someone orders for you and you're okay with it, fine, keep rolling. However, be aware this could be a sign of controlling behaviour. Ain't no man taking my decisions away from me!
2. People talking about how rich they are and dropping tacky little hints about their wealth on a first date is cheap. Very, very cheap.
3. If someone drags your chair closer to them when they don't know you, or invades your personal space on a first date, they are setting a precedent for bad behaviour and it will only get worse.
4. If you have just discussed a huge job or life decision, and they suggest something that would benefit them and is completely irrelevant to you and what you've just said, they are never going to support the decisions you make. If they have such little regard for you that they cannot even be supportive or excited for you on a first date, this person will never, ever encourage you; they only care about themselves.

5. If a date belittles you in any way, or laughs at you for wanting to contribute, you are always going to be seen as *just a girl* to them, someone without income or ambitions of your own. This works both ways: If a girl belittles a guy, this is not okay either. Both sexes have their own emotional triggers as does each individual person.

6. Lastly, if someone displays signs of jealousy about you not being free on their command, just NO. Control alert. Asshole alert. Other direction alert. Swipe Left!

STORYTIME:

Before the great social media obsession had settled fully into my bones, I met a guy at the pub. I would have only been 21 or 22 at the time. He called that night on my way home and asked me to go on a date with him the next night. I agreed.

Let's call this guy Freddy. Freddy picked me up and took me out for dinner which he paid for. We went for a walk on the beach afterwards; predictable, I know. Our date was coming to an end and he suggested we go back to his house. I reminded him it was a first date and that I wasn't like that. He asked another two times on the way back to his car. I finally agreed. I went back to his house and had sex with him. I convinced myself it would be okay and maybe we'd catch up again. He had mentioned his ex a number of times in our conversations that night, but I was too naïve to pick up on it. I did see Freddy again, but it was only for sex.

TAKEAWAYS:

There are only a few takeaways here, but they are big ones so pay attention:

1. If a guy buys you dinner, you **don't** have to have sex with him; you don't owe him anything. YOU DON'T OWE ANYBODY ANYTHING, let that sink in.
2. If a guy asks you one time, two times, ten times or any amount of times to have sex with them and you don't want to, you don't have to. Stick to your guns and your first instinct. Don't feel bad and don't feel obligated.

STORYTIME:

For a red flag parade bigger than during Chinese New Year, please read on. I had been chatting to this guy for a couple of weeks on a free dating site. I was vibing him, he was good looking, he seemed to have his head screwed on; the normal things I look for in dates. *He was not an ex criminal.* We agreed to meet for coffee at a place where I stupidly hadn't Googled thoroughly enough: It was closed.

My date, whom I will call Fredericko because I like the way the name rolls off my tongue, and I walked to a coffee shop which was open. On our delightful romantic stroll, which was full of giving each other disgusting pervy side glances (clearly thinking, oh yeah, he's alright, and her ass is hot), we had an interesting conversation.

He worked with immigrants whose visas had expired, or who were being deported for various reasons. I said to Fredericko, "That must be a challenging job," being the empathetic caring biatch that I am. His response was, "Nah I love it. I love getting the scum out of Australia." From the moment those words left his mouth, I knew the date was over, before it had even begun. I didn't have the balls to say what I wanted, like, "Fuck off you uncaring dick wad, enjoy your lack of empathy and lack of a date," before storming off and making a dramatic exit. (Although a dramatic exit for me would have led to me tripping along the way – thanks dad for my clumsy genes!)

Instead, we got to the café where Fredericko insisted on paying for my coffee. We sat down and started chatting, which was okay, even though in the back of my head I had a siren screaming DICKHEAD ALERT. The siren was blaring so loudly, it made it hard to concentrate. My list of dislikes was stacking higher and higher on our *delightful* date. He hated his dad, who was also apparently a deadbeat. Even after I told him that I didn't have my dad anymore as he had passed away recently, he displayed as much empathy as a bag of rocks. Instead, he continued bitching about his dad and declaring that the only reason his dad looked after him when he was a kid was to get child support payments.

As the conversation progressed, a guy walked by who recognised Fredericko and they started chatting. The chat went on way longer than I felt was polite and I learnt a few too many details sitting there awkwardly, fiddling with my spoon, until the guy left. I learnt that Fredericko hated his ex and, although he got to keep their house, he ended up living at home with his mum. I thought, *okay, no problem*, until I asked him how long he'd been at home, and he said, "Two years". It seemed he had no intention of moving out; he wanted to stay living with his mum even though he was on good money and had a house. I was confused. Why wouldn't someone want to be independent? Fredericko had an Apple watch, a Volkswagen with personalised number plates ... he was doing well for himself. Or was this a facade? I give zero crumpets if a guy isn't rich, but why stay living at home at 32 so you can buy personalised plates and an Apple watch rather than living like ... I don't know ... like an adult, standing on your own two feet?

He continued to tell me how his ex had left him with a lot of debt, took their dog, blocked his number and was a massive bitch.

I had no idea about their situation or how unfair it really was. What I do know is that there are always two sides to a story, and his stories felt very uneven. He always cast himself as the victim and he seemed unable to let any of it go. So much negativity for a first date. So much.

TAKEAWAYS:

1. If someone doesn't have empathy, that is likely to extend to you as well if you continue dating. Why wouldn't it? If you hate everyone around you and you're the victim and want to get the 'scum' out of Australia, how long until *you* become the scum or the problem?

2. Make sure you listen on a date; really hear what your date is saying. There was nothing positive about what my date was saying. Yeah, he was good looking, but so what? If everything that comes out of a person's mouth is negative, do you really want to surround your lovely self with that? He seemed like he needed to grow as a person.

3. Light-heartedness is your best friend on a date. Make sure you aren't the person on a date who is negative and thinks the world is against you. Show your funny side, have a sense of humour. Show the other person your good qualities.

4. If a person is bringing up their ex on a first date, that is it. It can go no further. Seriously, don't fucking bother wasting your precious time.

STORYTIME:

I have a friend whom I am going to call Clement for this story. Like so many 20-somethings before him, he got married to the wrong person, had a son, realised he was in the wrong relationship and called it quits on the marriage. Clement was back on the market after over six years of not dating and ready to see what would happen. He started with online dating sites and met a few interesting ladies. He went on a date with a girl I will call Bessy, whose profile consisted of two filtered head shots. Clement liked the way Bessy looked, enjoyed reading her bio and was happy with their conversations, so he suggested a meet up.

They arranged to meet for a drink and Clement sat waiting excitedly, looking like a kid waiting for cake. He spotted a girl at the bar who looked nothing like the girl in the photos yet was staring straight at him and started walking in his direction. Surely not, he thought, she was totally different to the girl in the photos; was this even the same girl? She kept her eyes fixed on him as she wandered over and said, "Clement". He tried to be positive and thought that maybe she would have a lovely personality, but he didn't feel attracted to her or the fact she had been so misleading with her profile.

They were having a drink and his phone, which was sitting on the table, rang but he politely didn't answer it (I'm betting 95% of 20-somethings would have). His screensaver, a photo of his son, appeared which caught the attention of Bessy. "Who's *the kid*?" she sniped, the words 'the kid' said with snarky emphasis.

Matching her tone Clement said, "*The kid* is my son, and he is absolutely amazing."

"Oh. Well he wasn't on your profile, that's a bit dishonest."

"Actually, he *was* in one of my photos. And while we are on the topic of dishonest profiles, you look nothing like any of your photos," Clement shot back. Bessy looked shocked, as though she couldn't believe what she was hearing. Clement was confused as to how she could be so surprised. He said, "I think it is time we end this date."

This story has a little dishonesty on both sides. Let's work through these. I met my friend Clement through online dating, so I know that although his son *is* in one of his photos, he does not specify that he is his son. In fact, in the section concerning children, he answers 'wants one day' rather than 'has and wants more'. A lot of people include their nieces and nephews in photos, so it is not unusual to have photos of kids on a profile, even if they aren't yours.

While I have never met Bessy, it sounds like her profile wasn't a true representation of her appearance. The problem with online dating is that it presents the opportunity to try some DIY 'self-improvements' with filters. There is even a new app which alters people's eyes to make them look much bigger and brighter. There are apps to make people slimmer, to change the shape of your face, to change your tan, to add more colour here and there. By the time you add a little flower halo or dog ears you are complete. At what point are you no longer you? Where do you stop? It's like the tattoo sleeve fad – people started with one and ended up with one million … and no money.

TAKEAWAYS:

1. If you aren't real and honest on your profile, there is no way meeting up will ever go past a first date.
2. Be comfortable in your skin – no matter what colour, shape, or size you are. Show *you* to your date, not what you want to look like.
3. Don't use filters to change your appearance. Seriously, what does this achieve? Wouldn't you rather someone see you and think, 'Wow that person is better looking in real life,' rather than, 'Um, they don't look like their profile'?
4. If you have kids, this is completely fine! Don't hide it, embrace it. People know up front if this is a deal breaker for them, and

if you aren't open about it before meeting up, it is going to seem dishonest. If there is a section relating to children, fill it out honestly. Yes, some people may not be comfortable dating people in certain situations, that is their decision to make. Conversely, you may not want to date someone who never wants kids, and that is a choice too. These choices need to be respected.

5. Present an accurate representation of you. Showcase yourself on your profile so that someone will like you for you, and not the version of yourself you pretend to be.

STORYTIME:

Another story from my good friend Clement. He had been having a nice little chat with a lovely young lass on a free dating website and they decided to meet up. He invited her to his house for their first meeting, then they agreed to catch the train into the city for a drink. In the car on the way to the train station, the girl, whom I will call Marilyn, had a few ciders while Clement drove. They got on the train where the conversation continued, and they were digging each other's vibes. Clement raved about his cute three-year-old son. Marilyn liked kids and was into Clement so pretended to listen as he dribbled on about his son, 'Oh my child is better than everyone else's child blah blah blah.' The train ride continued, and the conversation went as follows:

Marilyn: Oh, I forgot my emdies.

Clement: Don't worry about them, I will throw them out tomorrow.

Marilyn: No, my emdies.

Clement: Yeah, I'll get rid of the empties later.

Marilyn: No. My MDMA pills. So we can have a *really* good time.

That was the point at which Clement, a responsible adult and parent, realised he was out on a date with a drug taker. This was a total deal breaker for him.

Clement: I don't do drugs.
Marilyn: You don't? Really?
Clement: Um no, I am surprised you do, you're an adult.
Marilyn: I am surprised you don't.

After some back and forth, they continued with their night both knowing it wasn't going anywhere. They were stuck together for the time being, so made the most of it, but it was just a night full of awkward niceties and small talk.

TAKEAWAYS:

1. Again, for the 50 millionth time, meet in a public place. This person, who Clement now knows to be a drug user, knows where he lives. If they had met separately, this awkward, doomed date could have ended after one drink. Instead, they were stuck together until they caught the train back to Clement's house.

2. [Putting on my stern mum voice] Drugs are dumb! Not only was Marilyn taking them, but she tried to make Clement feel inadequate and abnormal for *not* taking them. Serious high school behaviour. Really, the last person you want to be around is some dumb ass who resorts to manipulation or peer pressure to try to change you and your strong morals.

STORYTIME:

Okay this story is unbelievable and completely fucked, but it legit happened I promise. It is about my friend Artie, who was new to online dating and this was his first online date ever. He had no idea what to expect or what the norm was. Free dating site, I might add.

Artie had been exchanging messages with Gertie for about a week when they agreed to go for a hike together, as a first date. They agreed to meet at Artie's house and head off from there. Gertie changed their plans at the last minute and decided she wanted to meet at a shopping centre instead (smart move Gertie, public place). Artie thought it was strange but went along with the change. He was waiting in their agreed-upon location when a strange man approached him. He thought, *Holy fuck, have I been cat fished?* The man introduced himself as he put his hand out to shake Artie's.

Bill AKA Random: Hi, I'm Bill, Gertie's friend.

Artie: Um, hi I'm Artie.

Bill AKA Random: Gertie was a lil' nervous to meet ya, so I decided it might be best if I met ya first.

Artie: Where is she?

Bill AKA Random: I'll just grab her for ya. Ya seem like an alright fella.

Bill brought Gertie to meet Artie and left them to go on their hike together. They jumped in Artie's car and chatted whilst driving to the starting point of their hike. They'd been walking for a while when Gertie decided to let Artie in on her violent past behaviour. She had a bad temper (to put it mildly), had restraining orders taken out against her, and she'd also been arrested before. Artie, like a champ, kept calm and started to direct them back towards the car. He dropped her off and thanked the dating gods that he hadn't been murdered.

TAKEAWAYS:

Well, where do I even start on this one?

1. I absolutely recommend a first meeting to be in a public place, one where you feel comfortable. I usually go to a café, as there are always people nearby if needed. Stay in a public place and do not go to a secondary or secluded location on a first date. Anyone can pretend to be someone else or a nice person for five minutes. This story could have been SO much worse.

2. If you're going to bring a friend because you feel uncomfortable with a situation, warn the other person first. It can be incredibly intimidating and strange to have a third person appear when it is unexpected, especially if you have changed the venue. If you feel more comfortable having someone with you when you meet your date for the first time, no dramas; but you need to communicate this to your date.

3. Gertie was upfront on the first date about her problem with violence; hats off to her for being honest. The problem was there was no escape for Artie when he felt uneasy in the middle of a secluded hike. If the date was in a coffee shop, he could have made a safe exit. Thankfully the situation didn't escalate and serves as a good warning: You really don't know who you're meeting.

STORYTIME:

My mate Alfie had a bit of an interesting encounter with a young lady named Beth, also from a free dating site. After a couple of days of chatting they decided it would be a good idea to meet up in person. They had a sweet little coffee catch up, nothing more. Not even a kiss goodbye as unfortunately there was no chemistry. Alfie left the date not really wanting a second one and wished Beth well on her future dating endeavours. A few days later something super strange happened; he started received some interesting text messages from her:

Beth: Hey, I'm pretty sure I got chlamydia from ya.

Alfie: That isn't possible.

Beth: Yeh 'tis, I got it from ya, I'm positive. You need to get treated.

Alfie: I don't have chlamydia.

Beth: Ya do, ya gave it to me.

Alfie: We didn't kiss, or even hug. Unless it can be passed through conversation, you got it somewhere else.

Beth: Oh, sorry. You're the guy I caught up with for a coffee, right?

Alfie: Yeah. We had coffee a few days ago.

Beth: Wrong person, please ignore.

TAKEAWAYS:

1. First and foremost, use a fucking condom. Seriously, if you go on that many dates and sleep with that many people that you don't know who you got the clap from, use a condom! No judgement: Bang as much dudes or gals as you're comfortable with, but don't get comfy with their STDs too. CONDOMS, CONDOMS, CONDOMS [in my sternest mum voice]. Also, regular STD checks. That is all.

2. If you're dating multiple people, don't be a dumbass and mix them up. Check before you hit send. It is so obvious, and yet

I am guilty of it too. You send a person the message, 'I hope your shoulder feels better,' only for them to ask what's meant to be wrong with their shoulder. The worst. Remember, or be smart and check. We all multi-date in this fantastic online world, and that is fine. But you've got to be on top of it, or it'll get on top of you – like the clap.

STORYTIME:

Alfie hadn't learnt his lesson from Beth and the chlamydia debacle and decided to give love another go on another free dating site. He connected with Jan, the two hit it off via messages and it was clearly meant to be. They arranged a lovely date where Jan was going to meet Alfie at his house. From there, the future lovebirds had plans to go out for dinner.

Alfie ironed his shirt, *at least the front of it,* and splashed on a little too much of his best aftershave. Looking schmick, he checked himself in the mirror on the way to answer the doorbell, already smiling. His smile dropped when he opened the door and realised the person in front of him was not the person he'd been chatting to. Alfie had to think on his feet, real quick, bang, bang.

Catfish Woman: Hey, Alfie?

Alfie: No, I think you have the wrong house.

Catfish Woman: This is number 42, isn't it?

Alfie: Uh nah, sorry miss, you have the wrong house.

Catfish Woman: Oh haha, I don't think I do.

Alfie: Yeah this is number 46. 42 is two houses that way.

Catfish Woman: Oh okay, thank you.

Alfie closed and bolted the door. He changed back into his sausage dog pyjamas and ignored the door when the bell rang

again. That is what I like to call a bullshit smackdown. Alfie –
one, Catfish – zero.

TAKEAWAYS:

1. If someone isn't honest with you, don't feel guilty with a bullshit smackdown. In this case Alfie pretended Jan was at the wrong house as she was clearly not the person in the photos. Misrepresenting yourself the way that Jan did is also known as catfishing. There are many ways to call someone on their crap. Telling them straight that they misrepresented on their profile is a good one. If you're non-confrontational that is fine too, just send them a message post-catch up. Let them know their behaviour wasn't acceptable and that's why they weren't getting a second encounter with your lovely self.

2. I am sure I said this earlier in the book – if not I will say it again. NEVER arrange a first date at your house or give them your address. You don't know who they are (case in point in this story); you could be chatting to any random psychopath and have no clue. You don't want that cray cray ju ju knowing where you live.

3. Iron your full shirt.

EIGHT
THE OLD FAKEROO: FIRST DATES

STORYTIME:

HAVE BEEN ON a number of dates where the person's profile portrays them differently to how they really are. Sometimes physically, sometimes about their education, and sometimes regarding their family. I had about three or four first dates in a row where the men had profile pictures that were not recent. There is no way they could have been recent, and not just one or two of the pictures either but all of them. One guy was previously a professional athlete; his photos showed a fit young man living a healthy life. This suited me because I live a healthy and active lifestyle and am attracted to others who are the same. I met the guy, and he was at least 20-30kgs heavier than his profile picture. It put me off immediately – not the fact that he was overweight, but the fact that he misrepresented his current self.

When I saw him waiting at the bar, I wanted to turn around and leave before he saw me. But I am polite, so I didn't do it. I sat through the whole date thinking, *I bet this guy never gets anyone agreeing to go on a second date* even though he was a perfectly nice guy. I had chatted to lots of guys who weren't exactly in shape, but they accurately represented themselves in the first place. I was attracted to their personalities as I am huge on people who bring the funnies; I am not attracted to people who are dishonest. It would be the same if someone online represented himself to be,

I don't know, a body builder, but had the upper-body strength of my nana and was unable to lift his glass of water.

This has also happened with people being dishonest about their level of education. Don't claim to have a degree or to have completed postgraduate studies if you have never achieved these things. Starting one degree or even ten degrees that you never finished because [insert sad sob story here] doesn't mean you are university educated. There is no selection option for uni drop out; while there is nothing wrong with being a uni drop out, *I did it twice,* don't claim otherwise. Again, I chat to/date people who aren't university educated and it doesn't bother me at all. What bothers me is the lying.

I have also met a few people whose profiles say they don't have children (rather than leaving this section blank which is an option). Upon meeting them, they admit that they have children. If you lie, you take away the other person's ability to make an informed decision based on honest profiles. If some people don't want to date a single parent, are they being judgemental? Who knows and who cares; it is a personal preference and if people want to avoid single parents and don't want to waste anyone's time, they should have the option to do so. To me, it is like someone claiming to have children in order to get a date with other single parents, but the child is made up. Before long we are into some serious Dr Phil shit which all could have been avoided if all parties were honest in the first place.

STORYTIME:

This date really pissed me off. To give you some context, let me pre-empt this by saying that I am someone who knows what she is about and I hate being questioned by someone who believes they know what I want/don't want better than me.

I had been chatting to this guy whom I will call Jasper. We decided to meet; he seemed normal, he was single, and as he was an engineer and I was also in the oil and gas industry, I thought we'd have a little in common. I suggested a coffee and he suggested a bar instead on a Saturday night. I hadn't mentioned at that point that I was basically a non-drinker, but wasn't bothered by those around me drinking, so I agreed.

We met at a popular bar; one which didn't smell like vomit or have sticky floors, so it was a promising start. He seemed nice, and he was very good looking as well which was an added bonus. We sat down by the window and Jasper asked me what I'd like to drink. I let him know that I'd love a soda water with some lime in it. The look he gave me was one of shock; I could read his expression without him saying a word and the gaze lasted a few seconds. He then asked, "A wine, right?" I ended up agreeing and said, "Sure, a wine will be fine." He brought me back a glass of red. As an almost non-drinker, one drink is my absolute limit when driving because I am a lightweight, and on a first date I would never go past this anyway. I slowly sipped my drink and as we started talking about our careers, our conversation went a little bit like this:

Ash: What kind of engineer are you?

Jasper: Well, kind of a co-ordinator of engineers.

Ash: So, like an engineering lead? That is impressive, what field are you in?

Jasper: It's more like I coordinate the engineers, not quite a lead.

Ash: So, you're not an engineer, you administrate engineers?

Jasper: Well, in a way, but I know most aspects of the engineering role.

Ash: If you did your engineering degree though, are you wasting your skills doing that?

Jasper: Oh, I didn't exactly do an engineering degree, I have just worked with engineers and the job is easy.

It suddenly dawned on me that Jasper completely misrepresented his education and lied on his profile. What else had he lied about? I continued sipping my drink and Jasper asked me if I'd like another one. Again, I asked for a soda water and again, I got the same dissatisfied glare and he asked if I wanted a wine. I held firm to my request for a soda water, and I offered to pay this time. Jasper went to the bar and returned with a wine for me and a beer for him. This time I returned the dissatisfied glare. I decided not to drink it. He got up and went to the toilet, so I took the opportunity to go to the bar to buy myself a soda water with lime, the drink I actually wanted. He came back and noticed my new drink. I hope he was embarrassed, but I am not sure he was. I left my second glass of unwanted wine untouched and waited for him to finish his beer.

When Jasper got up and asked if I wanted another drink, I let him know I wasn't keen and was ready to go home. Again with the dissatisfied stare. Reluctantly, he stood to go, but then he looked at his watch, realised it was still early, looked at me again and sat back down. I had had enough of his crap. I grabbed my bag, thanked him for the drink and walked out. I walked myself back to my car, which I don't normally recommend, but because I could sense he wasn't going to leave I had to put on my big girl pants and make tracks. Instant regret for not swiping left on this one. Catchya on the flip side dickhead.

When he asked me out on a second date and I politely refused, I imagined the same dissatisfied look on his face as when I refused the wine. It made me smile.

TAKEAWAYS:

1. Don't feel pressured into agreeing to something you don't want. You shouldn't have to justify why you do or don't want something. "No," should be the end of the conversation.
2. If someone guilts you into doing something on the first date or belittles your choice, that could indicate a pattern of behaviour that will continue. If they can get you to change your mind about one thing, why wouldn't they try to get you to change your mind about another?
3. The whole incident reminds me of peer pressure in high school. I didn't smoke but one of my friends did, and she asked me to have a smoke with her, so she wasn't doing it alone. That was a turning point for us; I had the cigarette that day but felt crappy about myself after it. I stood up for myself the next time she asked, and I learned how to set my boundaries: No matter what it is, if you don't want to do it, say no. If someone doesn't agree with your choice, that is their problem, not yours.

STORYTIME:

I found the absolute man of my dreams on a free dating site. It was love at first sight, I was sure of it. He was hunky, a million feet tall with dark hair and dark features, had a good job, and was Canadian so was going to have a really hot accent, right? Well, it turns out I would never know. After chatting online for a week, we planned a time and place to meet up at a café which I always frequent with first dates as it is large and well-spread. The last thing anyone wants on a first date is eavesdropping turds on the next table smugly whispering, "They're on a first date, hahaha, let's listen in, how awkward."

The date was set for 7:00pm and we had confirmed it the

night before (always confirm a date if you've planned it a few days earlier; things change quickly in the world of online dating). It was 7:05pm and I had the feeling the guy wasn't coming. I'd had the feeling all day and I usually trust my freakishly intuitive side, but this time I told myself not to be paranoid and that my gut wasn't always right. Well, turns out my gut **is** always right. I messaged my friend and told her that he was late, and I had a bad feeling about it. She insisted I wait and not to be cray as he was only five minutes late. So, I messaged my date to tell him I had secured a back table and the last set of Connect Four and I looked forward to kicking his butt. No reply. Crickets.

So, I sat there by myself, writing book ideas in my little floral nana-like notebook. I didn't even order a drink while I waited. 7:30pm; still crickets. I thought that maybe he mixed 7:00pm with 7:30pm, and I sent him telepathic messages, *Come to me hunky giant man of my destiny.* 7:35pm – I sent him a real message to check if he was okay as he hadn't shown up. *Just in case there had been an accident – yes, I know grasping at straws, but my poor ego.* 7:40pm – I got a reply. His message read, 'Oh, I am sorry, I haven't been feeling well all day. I should have let you know earlier. Typical guy LOL.'

What, earlier than 40 minutes past our 7:00pm date start time? NO FUCKING SHIT, you've had three quarters of a day to have made that shit known!

I replied, 'Okay, I hope you feel better soon,' then drove to my bestie's house, crying along the way while listening to sad songs, wondering if I had gotten uglier and that was why no one wanted to meet me anymore. What was wrong with me? [Obviously, nothing – I am amazing.] I told my bestie that I really liked him and our chats, so I would give him the benefit of the doubt. She wasn't happy about it, but we played giant Jenga and drank hot chocolate like the 30-somethings we were.

The next morning, I woke up pissed off. People don't stand me up, that doesn't happen. I am amazing – my pics are honest, my profile is honest and WTF is with the, 'Typical guy LOL'? That wasn't normal behaviour; that was just bad manners so don't put that down to a gender thing hunky dream man. So, I went to un-match him and the rageful version of myself cropped up. That is the side of me I keep hidden from the world as I am scared of being locked up or sent to hell, which is hotter than central Australia. So, I messaged him:

> 'LOL, yeah that is pretty funny you think it is a *guy thing* to stand someone up. Considering I am 31 and this is the first time it has happened to me I think it is just a *you* thing. Get some manners and next time send a message.'

I left it until I could see he was online, and then un-matched him before he had any time to reply. Boom. He got my raging moral side. He probably rolled his eyes and thought *women are crazy*. IDIOT. But I felt better.

TAKEAWAYS:

1. You cannot always tell if someone is self-absorbed or has bad manners when you first meet them. You do usually get a preview when messaging or chatting on-line, but sometimes you just can't tell.
2. There are many reasons why someone might stand you up, and none of them are your fault. You're not the problem. You're amazing, you're worth it; they are a Jerky McJerkface. If your profile picture is dishonest and the person sees you and realises your duplicity, then I might understand why they'd stand you up. However, I assume they'd still need to confirm your identity (unless you had a secret outfit code…).

3. Don't assume someone is your future partner from an online chat. You don't know them. What you feel meeting someone online and then meeting them in person are often two different things. When you feel the same in person as you did online then that is amazing and unique and good luck: I hope you buy many future dogs together.

4. If someone does stand you up, be kind first, and don't jump to conclusions; there could be a legitimate reason. Maybe their budgie got stuck in the vacuum cleaner. Wait until you have the whole story and if it isn't good enough and the dog ate their homework, then feel free to rage a bit but absolutely DO NOT meet them if the reason isn't acceptable. You are not a door mat and you don't want to exude the vibe that you are and start something this way. Will they show up at the wedding? Or did they have the sniffles because *typical guy, lol.* Get me?

AUNTY ASH'S LIST OF FIRST DATE ETIQUETTE

GENERAL FIRST DATE RULES I STICK BY
(AND SUGGEST YOU DO TOO)

1. Do not post on social media while on a first (or any) date.
2. Do not discuss ex-partners on a first date. However, if the other person brings it up you have no choice but to answer truthfully. Don't start a bitching war about exes. Capiche?
3. Do not bitch or vent about shitty people you know; the person is your date, not your therapist. Unless they actually are a therapist and, in that case, remember that I said not to use a person's profession to your advantage, especially on a first date.
4. Guys AND girls: Always offer to contribute towards the bill. May I remind you again that you do not want to feel like you owe anyone anything (and even if you feel you do, it doesn't make it true). Also, if you are a girl and offer to pay/contribute, it gives the guy the sense that you like to look after yourself financially and don't expect a free ride. If the guy insists on paying well hallelujah, you can use that $5 you would have spent on coffee and buy yourself some pantyhose for that second date – or a tub of ice-cream to stuff your face with if there is no second date.

NINE
WARNING SIGNS IN THE EARLY DAYS

HAVE DECIDED TO put this story into the 'Warning Signs in the Early Days' section even though it could easily fit into the previous section of first dates. This was my first ever online date when I was a knob jockey and ignored all the warning signs. If one of my friends had told me this story, I would have screamed, "WARNING, WARNING, WARNING!" This is a story where I could have been murdered like in one of those scary movies where you yell at the screen, "Why are you doing that?" [Why does the victim always do stupid stuff like go out the front of the house?] Don't get me wrong, it is never the victim's fault, EVER. I am merely telling you to take some preventative actions to minimise risk.

STORYTIME:

I had been chatting to a guy for a week or two. He seemed nice enough and suggested we meet up for breakfast. I thought this was a great idea and agreed to go. I was excited for my first date. All the normal things went through my mind: What do I wear? What will we talk about? Will he like me? Will I like him? When will we get married? Will he also want 12 children?

The conversation was quite pleasant and when I discussed my dream of wanting to get into the police force, he listened. He said he had some police shows that he had recorded and suggested we go to his house to watch them. I politely declined, explaining that I wasn't comfortable doing that on a first date (not that you need a reason beyond just saying no). That was the first potential warning sign missed. The second thing which I noticed, and should have paid more attention to, was the way he responded to a kid who accidently spilled some water on our table. He glared at the young boy, who was maybe seven years old, like he had stolen money out of his pocket … it's just water, calm your farm mate. He also didn't thank the waitress or even acknowledge her presence. That was so rude. I don't think there is ever a time when that sort of behaviour is okay. I should have taken more notice of it, or at least been annoyed by it enough to end the date straight after breakfast.

Next, and yes this legit happened, he suggested we go to a nearby walking trail for a wander. I agreed. But this was not the worst part. Firstly, instead of minimising my risk and driving there myself, I stupidly agreed to go in his car to the start of the trail. Secondly, I should have excused myself to go the bathroom and texted my support person to let them know where I was going and possibly his licence plate as well. That would have been a smart way to proceed. Of course, I didn't do that, or we wouldn't have this story full of warning signs.

So, I got into his car and we drove to the walking trail. We went for a wander and were chatting about Game of Thrones. I was shocked that he hadn't watched it yet and suggested he get with 2014 and jump on it. That was when he said, "I have the whole season back at my place, why don't you come and watch it with me?" Even though the warning sirens were blasting in my head loudly, I again laughed it off and said, "Not on a first date. It might be time for me to get back now." His reaction was short and ill-humoured; he seemed annoyed I wasn't falling for his sex trap. As he drove me back to my car, he said, "Oh I just need to get some petrol on the way," and he drove a street *past* where I was parked to the petrol station. I sat in his car waiting for him to get petrol and, at this stage, I should have used this opportunity to text my support person or gotten out of the car and walked. I didn't. I was stupid. It wouldn't have been my fault if that guy had turned out to be a predator – it is NEVER the victim's fault – but I could have taken some precautionary steps along the way. It was my first online date, and I was naïve. This book is to help you be less naïve than I was.

Back to the story ... he finished filling up and on the way back to my car, he said, "My house is on the way back to your car, why don't we stop and you can have a look?" I was losing patience but continued to be polite and said, "No thank you, it's time for me to get home." HE PULLED UP IN HIS DRIVEWAY AND TURNED OFF THE ENGINE! This is not a joke. This happened, legit happened. He then said, "Well, we're here now, you may as well come in for a look." I shouldn't have been shocked; I wouldn't have been had I recognised the previous warning signs. In a firm tone I said, "Take me back to my car, now." I should have gotten out and walked. I didn't. He finally listened and dropped me back at my car. It easily could have gone the other way, and it's clear that you only need to ignore the warning signs from the wrong person one time to end up in a bad situation.

TAKEAWAYS:

1. Do not get into someone's car on a first date. If you change venues, follow in your own car.
2. If someone invites you back to their home and you aren't comfortable with it (which I never am on the first few dates) be firm and say you're not comfortable. Don't pussy foot around. Don't be too polite; be assertive.

3. If you **do** get into their car (I strongly, STRONGLY discourage doing this), message your safety person all the information you have available to you: where you're going, the time, the licence plate of the person (a sneaky photo of their licence plate will do it) and so on.

4. When people are rude to waitstaff and/or children, they tend not to be nice people, and it's a turn off. (But if you are also the type of person who is rude to waitstaff and/or children, please feel free to go on that second date.)

5. If a person ignores your push back and continues with stupid suggestions and trickery to get you back to their house, say, "Thank you for the date, but I have to get going." No explanation needed. They can draw their own conclusions. Get up, walk out and feel great that you dodged a bullet. Potentially both a metaphorical and a literal bullet.

AUNTY ASH'S TOP RED FLAG LIST

1. Too much contact
2. Too little contact
3. Too many vain photos
4. Looking more interested in your boobs than your face
5. Bragging about money or status
6. Being insistent that you do something you don't want to
7. Making you say 'no' more than once
8. Lying on a profile
9. Asking for sex prior to meeting
10. Talking to you like you're an idiot

I could keep going but you're all smart enough to get it sooooo … SWIPE LEFT!

TEN
ONLINE STALKING

THIS SECTION IS well beyond me and I hadn't even thought to include it until I sat down and talked to some *younger* friends. I had run out of my own stories, plus I wanted perspectives from others, and that is when I got this gem of a story which concerns the hell out of me.

STORYTIME:

My friend, whom I am going to call Valerie, met a guy on a free dating site. They started talking, and that was the end of it for her. She had worked out quite early on that the guy, whom I will refer to as Clyde, was not the man of her dreams and she stopped communication straight away.

What Valerie hadn't realised or considered, was that her dating app was linked to her Instagram account. She had always thought of this as a positive as she enjoyed reading about other peoples' lives that way, so she did the same. One night, Valerie caught up with some friends after work at their local. They posted a hashtag adorbs pic of themselves all dolled up, no doubt red lipstick all around the table. In one of the pictures there was a name badge visible with their company details on it.

The next week, Clyde showed up at Valerie's work. Yep, you read that correctly; she had never met this guy, yet he managed to track her down by stalking her on her Instagram. And this happened weeks later when she posted that photo. He had been watching her movements for WEEKS….

TAKEAWAYS:

1. Know the settings of your social media accounts; be aware of what you are sharing with others.
2. Be very careful what you post. From break-ins occurring when you post your holiday snaps whilst poolside, to stalkers building their profile on you. You can attract the wrong kind of attention in a world where everyone wants their Kardashian moment of fame.

STORYTIME:

Remember my friend Walter? He was doing what every other Aussie traveller does and spent time in London – England's top spot for about 1 billion Aussie travellers … thanks for having us guys! While he was there, Walter met a really nice guy whom I will call Earnest. Like half of London's population, Earnest was doubling as a model, so not only was he ridiculously good looking, but he was also pretty sure of himself. Walter was so nervous, intimidated and excited for their date.

The pair met up at a nice restaurant and the temperature of the convo was flirty, with a touch of chilli. Walter was feeling it; not only was the guy mega hot, male model hot (obviously), but he seemed to be really engaged in the conversation. That was when Walter, unable to control his nerves, spilled a little beer on the table. Earnest didn't seem worried and the pair continued their awkward first date small talk, ordering another two drinks, some entrées and mains to seal the date with the noms.

Walter, feeling out of his league and caught up in a storm

of insecurity, accidently knocked over his second beer. This time the beer spilled all over his lap, including his man junk. So, he excused himself to go to the bathroom, which Earnest seemed fine with. Walter went to the bathroom and, as anyone else who gets ultra-sweaty knows, there are some serious bathroom manoeuvres you have to execute to use the hand dryer on certain body parts. After ten minutes of drying his man junk region, Walter went out to see if Earnest would be interested in continuing their chat/moving things along. Walter found the food ... but no date.

The embarrassed waitress came over to break the news that his date had left. That's right, Earnest had taken his hot little mod bod out of there, leaving not one dollar (or a pound) for the bill. Walter sat down with two entrées, and two mains on the way. Although he felt like an idiot, *which he was not*, the waitress sat down with Walter as she had just finished her shift. They ended up having the food and drinks that were meant for Walter and Earnest and got on so well they went on to have a few more dates after that and ended up as BFFs.

TAKEAWAYS:

1. Walter did nothing wrong; sometimes people get nervous.
2. Even though it is hard when something shitty happens, something brighter could be waiting.
3. Just because you're a model doesn't make you better than anyone else. If you aren't into your date, tell them; don't be a cruel asshole and leave them sitting in a restaurant on their own.

ELEVEN
THINGS THAT ARE ABSOLUTELY NOT OKAY

FRIEND DITCHING:

DON'T BE THE person who ditches their friends when they are dating someone. I have been guilty of doing this, and I'm telling you it doesn't pay off. My friends are by far the most successful relationships I have, so I am incredibly relieved I grew out of this phase. You need to identify which of your friends are toxic and stop socialising with them. Narrow it down to great friends; don't confuse the two. If something goes wrong with the relationship you ditched your true friends for, where does that leave you?

MOVING MORE QUICKLY THAN YOU'RE COMFORTABLE WITH:

Make sure that if you start dating someone you're interested in and they are moving too quickly for you, speak up. Let them know. It won't work out if they're sprinting for the finish line while you're dawdling along smelling the roses. If they don't listen, then it's a good sign they aren't on the same page as you and you may need to re-assess. Also take note if the person you're dating is trying to have this conversation with you. Remember; if they are talking to you about it, they clearly think that there is *something* there and they want to ease their way into feeling out what that *something* is. Not everyone's feelings work at the same speed. Different personalities, different types of people; we all work in unique ways.

MAKING ONE ANOTHER FEEL SHIT FOR BEING THEMSELVES:

Dating is harder for some people than it is for others. It is important to be kind; nobody is perfect. Be gentle with one another on the journey of finding the right person. Remember the old saying [and I'm rolling my eyes whilst writing this], 'If you don't have something nice to say, don't say anything at all'. This counts for messaging too.

PUSHING SOMEONE INTO, OR BEING PUSHED INTO, SOMETHING YOU DON'T WANT TO DO:

This could refer to anything and everything on a date. Going to a secondary location, meeting additional people, having sex, stealing meerkats from the zoo. Be respectful to the other person and, most importantly, be respectful to yourself. Speak up: Remember that you have a voice and learn to use it.

LEADING SOMEONE ON:

Don't do it, it's cruel. If you don't feel it but you just like the attention and someone taking you out, don't be selfish. It'll end badly. You may also be the one to be led on. Try to pick up on verbal and non-verbal cues and again, speak up, ask questions. Communication is an important tool to sort this one out.

TWELVE
FRIEND-PILLARS AND SURROUNDING
YOURSELF WITH GOOD COMPANY

HAVING RELIABLE AND trustworthy friends is so helpful when dating. You want friends who know you well, friends you can trust with your whereabouts on dates, friends who know your code for when you're in trouble. If you don't have a close friend you can trust with the responsibility of being your safety person, perhaps turn to a family member.

When you go on a date you want to give this trusted friend as much information as you can. Tell them who you're meeting and when, where you're going, when you'll be home, and a screenshot of your date's profile if you met them online. If at any point during the date you change locations, or go to a secluded place, make sure you update your friend. This is extremely important. Be safe; you're such an important person, and you don't want to put yourself at risk.

Having friends as pillars to rely on is fabulous when it comes to giving and receiving advice. I always find my friends are honest when it comes to who I am dating. Sometimes you make excuses to yourself for someone you like, but your friends won't do this if they have your best interests at heart. They should tell you, "Hey, that shit ain't right." Sometimes friends can give you the confidence you may not have in yourself. Or maybe you are that friend that gives others around you the confidence to stand up and say, "No deal".

THIRTEEN
AFTER DATE MANNERS

Sooooooo many things go through your head post-first date, right? Mine too. I always categorise a date as one of three types:

TYPE ONE: 'JUST NAH'

Just nah, nice enough but not feelin' it. Or just nah, weirdo. Or just nah, old fakeroo profile … let's call this type the 'Just Nah' group. If you get a 'Just Nah' on your first date, you tend to breathe a sigh of relief when you get the hell home and put your pjs straight back on thinking *I missed Gilmore Girls for this?* But what next? What if the guy or girl starts inboxing y'all like, 'You tick all my boxes.' I don't do ghosting – I find it rude and it doesn't really give the other person any closure. It hurts their feelings, and they wonder why they are being ignored.

If the person messages you wanting another date, be nice about it. Don't ignore them, tell them honestly how you feel. If a person messages me suggesting another meeting, I always say something like: 'Thank you for a lovely date, I didn't quite feel the spark I was hoping to find. Good luck meeting your perfect person.' I always find the message is nice and positive because you're wishing them well. If they come back angrily (a rare occurrence), that is when I block and ignore them. Usually niceness is met with niceness. If the person does not message at all after the date, then fair game, don't write anything as there is no need. NEXT.

TYPE TWO: 'YEAH MAYBE'

Let's call this group the 'Yeah Maybe' group. I had some dates where I thought, *he was nice, he seemed nervous but maybe on a second date there will be more attraction or sparks.* Or maybe I got on really well with the guy and although I didn't feel a spark initially, there was potential for one to grow. Online dating can be hard if you're used to the kinds of relationships where you're friends first. It seems that everyone is looking for instant love. What happens if you're someone who likes to ease your way into it? I am. The best relationships I have had are with people I was friends with for a long time first. We know that online dating can be tricky. If there is one thing I have learnt, you might not know if the connection is right straight away. So long as you are honest with the other person and you tell them you want to get to know them slowly, then you're fine. If they don't want to wait, then it's clearly not the right fit. Like my bra, which I like to stuff for extra effect.

In terms of manners with the 'Yeah Maybe' group, be upfront that you want to take things slowly. Even if they are really excited and over the top, maintain your own level of excitement. Don't pretend to be on their level. If they are good at reading subtle cues, it may help them to ease up a little. I have given an example below, so you understand what I mean.

Jim sent Rosalie a message before she had even gotten home after their first date, like a hell keen head. He said, 'Hey Rosalie, touching base. I had such a lovely time today. You tick all of my boxes ☺ When are you free to catch up next?' Rosalie felt bad because she knew that even though she was keen to meet up again, she didn't feel quite as enthusiastic as Jim. She didn't want to hurt his feelings, so she matched his level of excitement. She sent him a message that read, 'Hey Jim, I know right? I had the best time too. Felt like we really clicked. Are you free tomorrow night?'

A response like this, although it may have made Jim feel like he had a real shot with Rosalie, isn't very truthful and could be setting him up for a big letdown after a second date if Rosalie wasn't keen. Rosalie could have tried something like, 'Hey Jim, thanks for catching up. We could catch up again sometime next week, if you're free?'

Make sense? Just be you, and you'll be fine.

TYPE THREE: 'HELL KEEN'

Let's call this the 'Hell Keen' group. The word keen is something my mum uses when she talks about dating and she is in her fifties. She'll be 'hell keen' she got a mention. Anyways. These are the rarest kinds of dates, when you get that *OMG this could totes be my future husband* feeling in your gut. You feel butterflies and your special lady garden gets tingly and you are all obsessed, and you want to message him immediately. There are a couple of things you need to think about before you do that. Remember, the person you are obsessing over may have viewed your date as a 'Yeah Maybe' or a 'Just Nah' type of date. I don't believe in playing games; I want them to know I am interested. I don't want to seem too keen though, so I try to communicate at a 'Yeah Maybe' level of excitement to avoid coming off too strong. But if they contact you with a 'Hell Keen' response, then knock your socks off and match that level of excitement.

I hope this helps you break down dating types in your head. Consider your response before hitting send. Reply with respect, kindness and understanding. Every now and then you might get responses that you cannot make sense of whatsoever and that don't fit any of the above types. Remember this isn't on you. You just do you. Don't take on someone else's issues as if they are your own.

AUNTY ASH'S PROFILE HINTS AND TIPS

I am going to keep this section short and sweet as profiles are a separate topic altogether. I will focus on this more in one of my next books but in the meantime, here is a brief run down.

When you're writing your dating profile, you want it to reflect you. What do you like? What do you stand for? What are your hobbies? If it is clear you haven't put a lot of thought into your profile, why should someone spend the time reading it? If someone has the option to write about themselves and chooses not to, I always swipe left. I like to see if someone has a sense of humour or similar interests before wasting my time or theirs.

For example, I am an introverted non-drinker. If someone has hobbies such as frequenting pubs and always being out with friends, I wouldn't worry about reaching out to them. Does that make sense? That doesn't mean that I believe you need all the same hobbies and interests as someone you're dating. But it is good to have some common ground; like you're both introverted and like reading. You both like indoor hobbies. You both enjoy outdoor sports. Neither of you like clubbing. You both like clubbing. You are both social and outgoing and have FOMO (Fear Of Missing Out). You both have FOBI (Fear Of Being Included). You both like stealing parts of your neighbour's succulents and denying it's theft because it grows back. You see what I am saying here? You don't want to waste anyone's time. Write a smidge about yourself and you'll probably match with some awesome people you have a few overlapping things in common with.

Photos, photos, photos. My biggest irk on people's profiles. Be fricken truthful. Be yourself. Don't be a faker. Post current and interesting photos. Don't post vain selfies without your shirt on, unless you want to attract other vain people … then knock yourself out with that crap. Don't put photos of you from five years ago, you're wasting everyone's time. Don't make shit up. The truth will come out and again, it wastes everyone's time. DON'T USE FILTERS. In real life there are no filters. Enough said.

I find action photos of you doing your hobby will always be alluring. You drinking a coffee because you're a coffee lover. You walking your dog because you're a dog lover. You browsing in a bookstore because you're a bookworm. You on a jet ski. You camping. You gardening. You using cotton buds to clean your skirting boards because you can't stand dust particles. Got it?

Do not sit there and list all the things you hate about the other sex. Worst idea. Stop whinging. We have all been burnt before, *get some sunblock*. We don't need to know that you clearly want someone completely different to your ex-partner. That is on you to do some vigilant swiping. The worst thing is when you find a hell juicy fish that you want to lure but they are completely put off by your shitty attempt at bait. Bait better people! Use the good candy on the hook.

FOURTEEN
BEING READY TO BAIT AND CAST YOUR LINE

ARE YOU REALLY READY?

YOU ARE THE most important person in your life. You **must** come first. You need to ask yourself some important questions before heading out there to find your trolley full of candy.

Questions to ask yourself:

AM I READY TO DATE?

Are you in a good place, in a place of self-love? What will you give another person? What will they give you? Are you willing to share the attention of your adorable cavoodle with another person?

WHAT DO I WANT TO GET OUT OF DATING?

Set an expectation for yourself. Then you'll know whether you're looking for something casual, serious or in-between.

WHAT VALUES DO I WANT IN A PARTNER?

If you know what you're looking for, it can be easier to block out the noise and focus on that. At the same time, you don't want to get dating-tunnel vision. Balance is important.

WHAT ARE MY DEAL BREAKERS?

If you don't want to date someone with dogs, then don't. If you don't want to date someone whose favourite colour is green, then don't. If you only want to date financially secure people, then do that. If you only want to date people who are studying, then do that. You have choices, so make them.

Okay daters, I am going to leave you to get your groove on. I hope this book has helped you in some way with your dating futures. I really wish I'd had something like this to push perspective into my life and to cut through some of the crap of dating early on.

Remember sometimes you may go on 100 first dates and not meet anyone you feel a connection with. This is okay. Don't settle. The wait will be worth it, no matter how long that is. Because who doesn't want a trolley full of candy?

www.ingramcontent.com/pod-product-compliance
Lightning Source LLC
Chambersburg PA
CBHW072146020426
42334CB00018B/1899

* 9 780645 040418 *